SWIPE RIGHT ON STOCKS

YADNESH CHAVAN

NewDelhi • London

BLUEROSE PUBLISHERS
India | U.K.

Copyright © Yadnesh Chavan 2024

All rights reserved by author. No part of this publication may be reproduced, stored in a retrieval system or transmitted in any form or by any means, electronic, mechanical, photocopying, recording or otherwise, without the prior permission of the author. Although every precaution has been taken to verify the accuracy of the information contained herein, the publisher assumes no responsibility for any errors or omissions. No liability is assumed for damages that may result from the use of information contained within.

BlueRose Publishers takes no responsibility for any damages, losses, or liabilities that may arise from the use or misuse of the information, products, or services provided in this publication.

For permissions requests or inquiries regarding this publication, please contact:

BLUEROSE PUBLISHERS
www.BlueRoseONE.com
info@bluerosepublishers.com
+91 8882 898 898
+4407342408967

ISBN: 978-93-6261-086-7

Cover design: Rishav
Typesetting: Sagar

First Edition: October 2024

Contents

Preface 1

Plot 5
The Plot: Love and Ledgers on a Banker's Date

Chapter 1 9
The Monetary Policy Interwoven Threads: Navigating Love and Loans

Chapter 2 25
The Stock Market Volatility Cricket, Crockery, and Common Ground

Chapter 3 39
The Journey Beyond Numbers, Designs, and Quantitative Easing (QE)

Chapter 4 55
Lessons from the Heart - Navigating Behavioral Finance through Kabir's Tale

Chapter 5 89
Yields of Affection: Navigating the Bonds of Love and Finance

Preface

The idea behind "Swipe Right on Stocks" came from a simple observation that most people find traditional investing advice too boring or confusing, so I wanted to make it simple and relatable. I wanted to change that by using contemporary language and styles with the basics of stock market investing. With over two decades of experience managing investments in many different asset classes through the ups and downs of markets. Along the way, I've realized how daunting financial concepts can be for many. That's why I decided to write something different—a book that explains these ideas clearly and in a way that's easy to relate to. Through this book, I've told the story of Arjun and Meera, two characters who, like many of us, are trying to juggle their careers and personal lives. Arjun works in finance, while Meera is in the creative world of fashion. Through their experiences, you'll learn about managing investments, understanding risks, and making smart financial decisions.

The aim of this book is straightforward: to help you understand finance in a way that makes sense for your life. Whether you're just starting to invest or you've already dipped your toes in the market, the lessons in this book are meant to be practical and easy to use. I believe that knowing about finance is crucial for empowerment, and I want to make sure everyone has the tools they need to make smart money choices.

As you follow Arjun and Meera's story, you'll see how the choices they make in their personal and professional lives can teach us all something about the financial decisions we face every day. I hope you'll find that learning about finance doesn't have to be difficult—it can be as simple as the everyday choices we all make.

Writing the book wasn't just about teaching financial concepts—those are things you can easily find online. Instead, I wanted to ignite a deeper interest in the younger generation: a realization of why understanding the financial markets is so important. In a world where everything is just a swipe away, it's easy to ignore the value of economic knowledge. But the truth is, these markets affect our daily lives, from the price of our morning coffee to the stability of our future. My goal with this book is to connect with young readers on a personal level, to inspire them to look past the jargons and see that financial analysis isn't just for Wall Street—it's for anyone who wants to take control of their life and future. It's about sparking curiosity so that the next time you swipe, it's towards a more informed and empowered version of you.

Thank you for picking up "Swipe Right on Stocks." I hope it gives you useful insights and helps you feel more confident in managing your money. With the right knowledge, anyone can take charge of their financial future.

Plot

The Plot: Love and Ledgers on a Banker's Date

In my career in banking, the market's relentless rhythm sets the pace, showing little mercy. I spent hours engrossed in financial models and complex reports, focused on numbers and predictions. When I left work, the sky was painted with orange and pink hues, marking the end of another day governed by economic tides.

But that evening was not about balance sheets or market trends; it was about Meera. She had picked a serene rooftop restaurant in the city's busy hub for our date. This place seemed to float above the chaos. I approached the receptionist and told him my name. "I am Arjun. We have a reservation tonight." The receptionist led me to our seat. I couldn't help but be captivated by the sight of Meera. She was dressed in a creation from her latest fashion line, showcasing her creativity and sense of beauty. The dress was a vibrant, captivating piece, much like Meera herself.

"You look worn out Arjun. Tough day?" she asked.

"Yeah, there is an RBI MPC meeting on Friday, and much action from RBI is expected. Making a profit from trades in this uncertain environment is tough, you know," I replied while attempting to grin but my fatigue was visible.

"You're not alone. Tell me about it. I won't pretend to understand all the banking jargon, but I know when you're stressed." She reached across the table, her hand gently squeezing mine—the ambient music blended with the light talk, surrounding them to create a soothing backdrop.

"It's just... these decisions have a big impact. The policy changes could affect the market for months, maybe years."

"And yet, here you are, with me. I'm impressed. Most would carry the weight of the world on their shoulders."

I look into her eyes, the stress lines easing on my face. "With you, I can put down that weight, even if it is just for a moment."

Meera smiled, her eyes reflecting the candlelight.

"You look beautiful, by the way. That dress... it's one of yours, isn't it?" I asked.

She smiled. "Guilty as charged. I wanted to wear something special tonight."

The food arrived, and we began to eat and the conversation flowed effortlessly. Meera talked about her fashion house, the challenges, and the small victories, while I listened intently. "Your world it's so different from mine. So full of colours and creativity. It's refreshing." I Spoke.

"And your world is all numbers and strategies. But you know, they're not so different. We both take risks, we both create something."

I nodded as a new awareness dawned on me. "I never thought of it that way. Our "creations" are less tangible in banking, but the impact is real."

"Exactly. Whether it's a financial policy or a fashion line, we're both shaping the world," she replied.

As we parted ways that night, I realized that Meera and I were weaving our unique stories, one thread at a time, into the grand tapestry of life.

Chapter 1

The Monetary Policy Interwoven Threads: Navigating Love and Loans

It had been a month since the evening on the rooftop, and Meera and I had both been very busy with our work. Meera had been busy getting ready for a fashion show, working with fabrics and meeting with clients, using her great design skills. At the same time, I had been dealing with financial analysis and meeting with clients due to changes in interest rates by the RBI. These changes had brought both challenges and opportunities in the banking sector.

Amid our busy schedules, we had managed to steal moments of connection, often over calls that served as brief escapes from our demanding routines.

"Hey, Meera. How's the evening treating you?" I asked on one of our calls.

"I just wrapped up a series of fittings," Meera replied. "The new collection is coming together, but it's a race against time. What about you?"

I chuckled lightly. "It's been a busy time. The increase in interest rates has caused a lot of volatility. We've had many meetings to plan and have talked to clients. It's fascinating to learn about how the financial market operates."

"Speaking of dynamics, the fashion show is next week," Meera said. "I wish you could be there. It's shaping up to be quite the event."

"I wish I could, too. Your shows are always a highlight. How's the final preparation going?" I said.

"Well, it's a mix of chaos and creativity. Last-minute changes, final touches on the outfits, and coordinating with the team. It's exhausting but exciting," Meera responded.

"You always manage to pull it off brilliantly. Your creativity never ceases to amaze me. So, anything new besides the fashion show?" I inquired.

"Actually, yes. I received a letter from the bank today about the Mudra loan, but I'm not entirely clear about it. I will email it to you; could you have a look?" Meera responded.

"Yes, for sure, my love" I said

"I appreciate it. Diving into these financial documents isn't exactly my cup of tea." Meera said.

I smiled. "I understand. That's what you have me for, right? For navigating these financial waters."

Meera shot me a playful grin, her eyes sparkling. "Of course you are. My own personal financial genius. How did I get so lucky?" she added with a cheeky wink.

"Always here for you, Meera. Let's tackle this together. And hey, we'll discuss it over coffee this weekend. How does that sound?" I responded.

"Sounds like a plan. I'm already looking forward to it.

The Love Letter...

Lying on my bed, with the echoes of my call with Meera still lingering, I had been lost in thought when a new email notification caught my attention. Meera had forwarded a letter from her bank. The subject immediately grabbed my interest—it was about the reset of interest rates on her Mudra loan, a crucial financial lifeline for her thriving fashion house.

As I scrolled through the email, the contents were just as I had expected. The bank had increased the interest rate, a standard procedure in response to the RBI's rate hikes. There was nothing unusual in the letter, just the typical jargon banks used. I planned to discuss it with Meera when we next met, knowing it might require some time to thoroughly explain and ease her concerns.

As I put away my phone, a different idea struck me. What if I wrote Meera a love letter? Not an email or a text, but an actual handwritten letter. There was something timeless and deeply intimate about putting pen to paper, a stark contrast to the fleeting digital communications that filled our days.

I grabbed a notebook, feeling slightly out of practice. How do you begin a love letter? "Dear Meera," I wrote, and then paused. How could I possibly express everything she meant to me and how our lives had intertwined, in mere words?

The Meet and the Rate Hikes..

Walking into Starbucks, I immediately noticed Meera sitting in our usual spot. The gentle ambient lighting bathed her in a way that always took my breath away. She glanced up, her grin familiar and warm.

"Hey there," I greeted, sliding into the chair across from her. "You're looking wonderful."

Meera gave a small, preoccupied smile. "Thanks," she replied. "How's your day been?"

"Good, now that it's ending with you," I said, trying to lighten the mood. We exchanged pleasantries and talked about our daily lives, but the tension was palpable.

I decided it was time to address the elephant in the room. "I saw the email about your Mudra loan," I began cautiously. Meera's face clouded with concern.

"Yes, that," she sighed. "I'm really stressed about it. They've increased the interest rate, and it's going to eat into my profits. I don't know if I can sustain the business if it goes up too much."

I could hear the fear in her voice, and it pained me. I reached out, covering her hand with mine. "Let's talk it through," I said softly. "I'll explain what this means in the simplest way possible."

"Meera," I started, choosing my words carefully, "imagine our country's economy as a huge, complex engine. This engine needs constant fine-tuning to run smoothly. The Reserve Bank of India, our central bank, acts like an expert mechanic who adjusts this engine using various tools. One of these crucial tools is the monetary policy."

Meera's eyes met mine, a mixture of interest and anxiety in them. "But why increase interest rates?" she asked, her voice tinged with concern.

"Let's talk about inflation," I said. "In simple terms, inflation is the pace at which the overall level of prices for goods and services rises, causing the purchasing power of the rupee in your hand to fall."

"High inflation is typically defined as 'too much money chasing too few goods.'"

Meera leaned forward and listened closely. To clarify the notion, I reminded her of her first love: mangoes, her favourite fruit.

Meera eagerly anticipated enjoying the delicious, sweet mangoes that signified the start of summer each year. With ₹500 in hand, we set out to the local market. However, as she strolled through the vibrant stalls, Meera noticed the prices had risen significantly, and she could buy fewer mangoes than the previous year.

Too much of money chasing too few goods

"Inflation affects everything—from groceries to the raw materials for your designs," I further explained.

Meera's eyes widened in realization. "So, it directly impacts my business costs and the budget of my customers."

"Exactly," I said. "Now, this is where the central bank's monetary policy comes into play. When inflation is high, the central bank may increase interest rates to encourage saving over spending. When customers save more and spend less, the demand for goods and services falls, slowing price increases."

"But doesn't that mean customers will spend less on things like clothes and accessories?" Meera asked with a hint of worry in her voice.

"Yes, that is a possible outcome," I acknowledged. "It's a delicate balance. The central bank's goal is to maintain inflation at a tolerable level—not too high to undermine the value of money, and not too low to cause a lack of spending. It's about finding the sweet spot where the economy expands smoothly without overheating." I grabbed a tissue paper and drew a simple diagram to describe the monetary policy.

RBI

To Control Recession	To Control Inflation
→ Repo rate cut	→ Repo rate hike
→ Interests rates drops	→ Interests rates increases
→ RBI needs to pump more money in market	→ RBI needs to pump out money in market
→ RBI buys govt. securities from banks to release liquidity	→ RBI sells govt. securities to banks to reduce liquidity
→ Result is more money with banks	→ Result less money available with banks
→ Cheaper money so that people take more loans and helps in controlling recession	→ people take less loan so money in market decreases, which helps in controlling inflation
→ Increased money supply may speed inflation	→ Rising interest rates curb inflation

I paused for a moment to ensure Meera was following. She watched closely, trying to grasp the complexities of the financial world, which was so different from the creative chaos of her design business.

"Meera," I spoke in a warm and patient voice, "Imagine the economy as a vast, intricate garden, where the RBI is the gardener, tasked with keeping everything flourishing."

I started with the Repo Rate. "Think of the repo rate as water for the plants. When the garden is dry, the RBI 'waters' the banks with lower repo rates, making borrowing cheaper. This allows them to lend at a cheaper rate to businesses and individuals, nurturing growth."

What is Repo Rate?

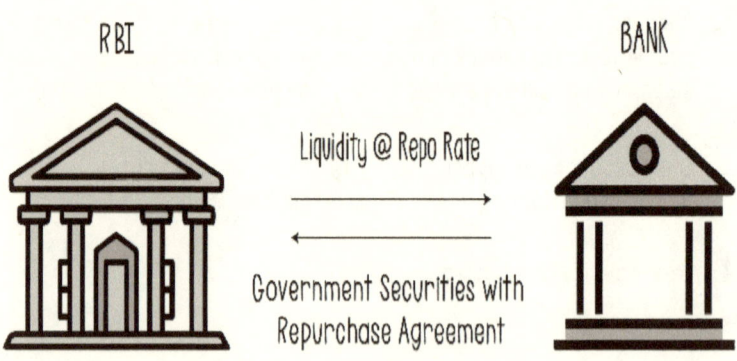

"The repo rate is the interest rate the RBI charges banks when they borrow money from it. If the RBI wants to make it more expensive for banks to borrow money—maybe because there's too much money floating around in the economy—it increases the repo rate. If the RBI wants to make borrowing cheaper, to encourage spending during a slow economy, it lowers the repo rate.

"Now, let's talk about the Standing Deposit Facility (SDF) Rate. Think of a situation where gardeners have excess water. The SDF Rate is like a special tank where they can store that excess water. The Reserve Bank, our water supplier, gives them a little reward, or interest, for this facility. It's a bit like a water savings account for gardeners."

The Marginal Standing Facility (MSF) Rate is like an emergency water service. If a gardener needs extra water urgently, they can get it from the supplier at a higher cost, using some of their precious plants as collateral. It's a bit more expensive than the usual water borrowing rate."

Finally, the LAF Corridor is like the range of water management options available. The MSF rate is the maximum, like a ceiling, and the SDF rate is the minimum, like a floor, with the repo rate sitting nicely in the center."

Main Liquidity Management Tool: The Reserve Bank sometimes organizes a big water distribution event every two weeks, where gardeners can bid for the water they need. It's like a major watering schedule that keeps everything running smoothly.

"Fine-Tuning Operations: These are minor tweaks to the irrigation schedule. If there's an unexpected hot or wet day, the Reserve Bank adjusts the water supply to keep all the gardens happy."

Meera nodded, her eyes reflecting understanding as I continued. "Now, the Reverse Repo Rate is like collecting excess water. When there's too much liquidity, the RBI uses this tool to absorb the extra funds, ensuring the garden doesn't flood."

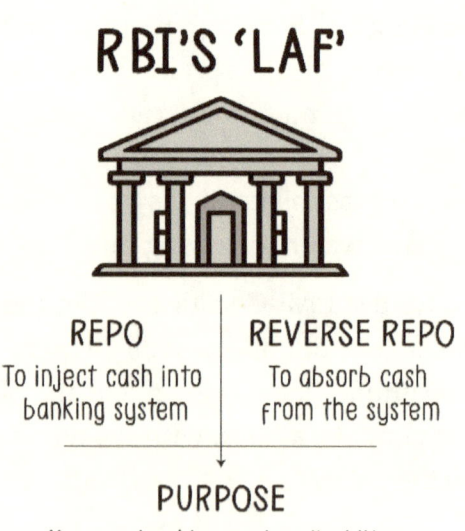

"This is the opposite of the Repo Rate. It's the rate at which the RBI borrows money from the banks. When the RBI wants to pull excess money out of the system, it offers a higher Reverse Repo Rate, enticing banks to park their money with the RBI instead of lending it out.

"Bank Rate: Imagine a gardener who doesn't maintain their garden well and needs emergency help. The Bank Rate is like a penalty for these gardeners when they need urgent water or plant care. It's higher than usual to encourage gardeners to take better care of their gardens."

We then touched upon the Cash Reserve Ratio (CRR). "CRR is like a reservoir. Banks set aside a portion of their deposits in this reservoir. When the RBI adjusts the CRR, it determines how much water is available to plants, influencing how much banks may lend."

"The CRR requires each bank to hold a certain percentage of its deposits in reserve, either as cash in its vaults or as deposits with the RBI. This ensures there's always enough cash in case many people want to withdraw their money simultaneously. Adjusting the CRR can control how much money banks have available to lend."

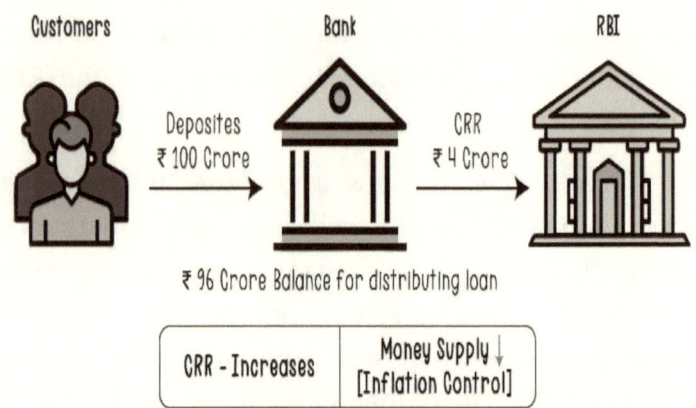

"The Statutory Liquidity Ratio (SLR) works similarly," I added. "It's like a backup water supply. Banks keep a certain amount in safe, liquid assets, ensuring they can meet their obligations without panicking."

"The SLR, which is similar to the CRR but has a broader scope, requires banks to hold a portion of their deposits in secure, liquid assets such as government securities. This is another method to prevent banks from running out of cash."

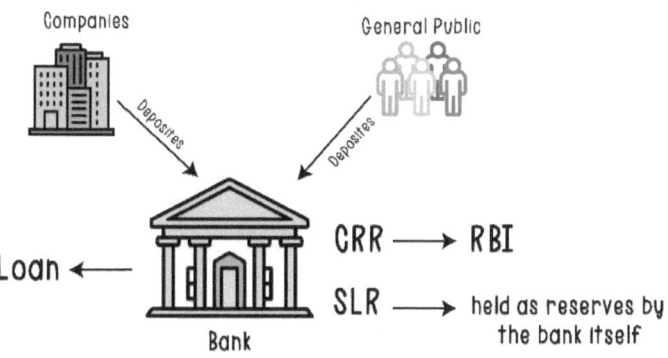

SLR - Increases	Money Supply ↓ [Inflation Control]
SLR - Decreases	Money Supply ↑ [Growth Booster]

"The Marginal Standing Facility is like an emergency water hose," I explained. "Banks use it to borrow funds overnight at a higher rate, which is useful during sudden dry spells."

"Banks can borrow money from the RBI overnight at the MSF rate, which is often higher than the repo rate, as a last resort when they need cash. Consider it an emergency lending facility for banks."

"Finally, we discussed the Market Stabilization Scheme. Think of it as a mechanism to drain excess rainfall, keeping the garden from becoming soggy. It helps in maintaining overall liquidity."

MARKET STABILISATION SCHEME (MSS) BONDS

- is a monetary policy intervention by the RBI to withdraw excess liquidity

- are special bonds floated on behalf of the government by the RBI

- are mostly shorter-tenure bonds

- money raised under MSS is kept in a separate account called MSS account and not parked in the government account or utilised to fund its expenditures

Meera, listening intently, offered a faint, approving smile. "Arjun, you've made it seem so easy and lovely. I never imagined the world of finance could be compared to a garden."

As we enjoyed our coffee, we found that discussing monetary policy in everyday language made it easier to understand. It became clear that using comparisons and storytelling could help demystify finance.

… Chapter 2

The Stock Market Volatility Cricket, Crockery, and Common Ground

Navigating a new phase in our relationship, Meera and I adapted to the changes around us. One evening, as the day drew to a close, Meera called me. Her voice was filled with concern.

"Hey, Arjun," she began, a touch of nervousness in her voice. "My dad is upset about the stock market. He's been involved in trading, but things haven't been going well lately."

I paused for a moment, aware of her father's somewhat strict attitude toward me. "What if I swing by this weekend? I could talk to him about the market. It might be difficult, given that he's never been my greatest fan, but it could help, you know?"

Meera responded with a mix of enthusiasm and caution. "That could be interesting, Arjun. Just tread lightly, okay? Dad's a bit set in his ways, and, well, you know how he's always been about us."

I smiled, appreciating her concern. "Got it. We'll keep it light and casual. It's just a friendly chat about the market. Who knows, maybe I'll win your father over with my charm and brilliant market insights," I joked, trying to ease the tension.

Meera chuckled. "That's the spirit! Be yourself, Arjun. That's the person I fell for, and I'm sure Dad will come around soon."

This weekend could add a new, promising future to our story, bringing me closer to Meera and her family. As we ended the call, I felt both nervous and excited; this wasn't just about market talk. It was an opportunity to break the ice between her father and me, and to show him the depth of my feelings for Meera in a subtle way.

The Weekend...

When the weekend arrived, I walked up to Meera's family home. Despite the beauty of the day, my stomach was doing flips. I had sensed her dad's stern demeanour, especially towards me, but I was determined to make the best of it.

The welcome was exactly what I had mentally prepared myself for—awkward, to say the least. Meera's dad shook my hand with a firm grip that seemed to last a bit too long, his face giving away nothing. The air was thick with formality, and I couldn't help but feel a bit out of place.

We settled into the living room, which was as posh as I had imagined. My eyes wandered over the elegant decor, the art pieces on the walls, the books that filled the shelves, and the family photos that were obviously of a rich, loving history. It was a beautiful space, but right then, it felt rather scarier than welcoming because of the elephant in the room.

Sitting on the edge of the sofa, I tried to lighten the mood. Meera looked at me and gave me an encouraging smile, which helped to make the slightly tense atmosphere more comfortable.

Mr. Kapoor sat across from me, looking like he was evaluating me. The room was quiet, the kind of silence that was heavy with unsaid words and expectations. I cleared my throat, reminding myself I was here to connect, not just as Meera's boyfriend, but as someone who wanted to win her family's confidence.

Meera, feeling the building tension, broke the quiet just as I was ready to start talking about something safe. "Dad, did you catch the cricket match last night? Virat scored his 50th century! What a game for Team India in the World Cup, right?"

Her father's face brightened up immediately. "Yes, I did! What an inning it was. Kohli truly is certainly a maestro of the game. His form has been outstanding in this World Cup."

I jumped into the conversation with relief, "His performance was excellent. It's incredible to see him play at this level." Meera's clever subject change worked wonderfully, reducing the initial awkwardness.

With a mischievous glance in my direction, Meera decided to steer the conversation towards my professional expertise. "Speaking of outstanding performances, Arjun works with a bank and is quite the stock market whiz. He could offer some important insights, especially considering the recent market fluctuations."

As I listened to her words, I sensed a sudden change in the atmosphere of the room. Her father's face transformed, his earlier warmth giving way to a stern look mixed with surprise and disapproval, as her comments lingered in the air. I then realized that Meera's well-intentioned pitch might have been too direct.

I raced to save the situation, "Sir, I'm still learning the ropes myself. There's always more to learn in finance, and I'd be happy to offer whatever ideas I have and hopefully learn from yours."

As I waited, the room fell into an uneasy silence. I hoped my words would ease the tension and allow a more open and collaborative discussion.

During a tense moment, Mr. Kapoor, Meera's father, finally relaxed. Our hearts, filled with anticipation and worry, was waiting for his response. His expression softened a bit, and he started to talk about what was bothering him. "The stock market has been quite unforgiving," Mr. Kapoor started, his voice carrying a hint of frustration. "Most of my trades haven`t fared well."

He paused for a moment as if contemplating his following words. "And, well, I've been trading based on tips I receive on WhatsApp. I thought they were reliable, but they've led to substantial losses. It's been a tough year."

I listened attentively, understanding the gravity of his situation. Trading based on unverified tips could be risky, and the volatile market had taken a toll on his investments. Further, Mr. Kapoor added, "My long-term holdings and mutual fund investments also have not performed well. In many situations, returns are negative or in the low single digits."

As Mr. Kapoor shared his concerns about his stock market investments and the substantial losses he had suffered from trading on WhatsApp tips, I pondered for a moment, searching for the right analogy to put his situation into perspective.

"Mr. Kapoor," I began, "You mentioned Virat`s 50th ODI century earlier. His career offers an excellent analogy for understanding the stock market. While Virat is a legendary cricketer, his performance has ups and downs. For instance, he didn't score any centuries in 2020 and 2021. In fact, in five out of his 15 years in cricket, he scored fewer than three centuries each year."

I observed Mr. Kapoor's attention sparked, as well as the curiosity of a cricket fan. "Yet," I said, "Despite these variations, Virat is regarded as one of the greats. Why? Because, throughout his career, he has maintained an amazing average and consistently strong performance. His long-term record, rather than his year-to-year achievement, solidifies his stature."

Drawing the parallel, I shifted the focus back to investing. "Similarly, in the stock market, there are years like 2022, where Nifty returns were modest at around 4.0%, and years like 2008, 2011, and 2015, where returns were negative. However, when we look at the long-term trend, equities have returned an average of 14% to 15%. Long-term trends are more important than short-term variations."

Mr. Kapoor listened intently as if the comparison struck a thought. "So, you're saying my focus should be on the long-term performance rather than getting swayed by short-term setbacks or unverified tips?"

"Exactly," I affirmed. "Just as Virat's legacy isn't defined by a single match or a bad year, your investment strategy should be focused on long-term growth and stability. Diversifying your portfolio and relying on research-based strategies, rather than short-term tips, will help you navigate the market's inevitable ups and downs better."

"Mr. Kapoor, when we talk about a research-based approach to investing, fundamental analysis is a key part of it. Let's take cricket as an analogy again. Selectors do not choose players for the national team based just on one or two strong performances. They evaluate the player's technique, fitness, consistency, performance under pressure, and much more over a period of time. Similarly, while doing fundamental research on equities, investors do not only look at the stock price. They delve deeper to understand the company's true value."

I paused for a moment to ensure Mr. Kapoor was following, and then continued, "Fundamental analysis involves evaluating a company's financial statements — like the balance sheet, income statement, and cash flow statement — to understand its financial health. But it's more than just numbers. It also involves understanding the company's business model, its competitive position in the industry, the quality of its management, market trends, and even macroeconomic factors like interest rates and economic growth."

Meera's father nodded, so I went on, "For example, if we consider a company - 'XYZ', a fundamental analysis would involve assessing how well it's managed, how it makes money, its growth prospects, how it stands against its competitors, and how external factors might affect its business."

"The goal," I concluded, "Is to determine whether a company's stock is undervalued or overvalued. This can help you make informed decisions regarding whether to buy, hold, or sell the stock. It's like betting on a cricketer's long-term potential rather than just one season."

"Mr. Kapoor, let us discuss ratio analysis, an essential component of fundamental analysis. Ratio analysis involves using key financial ratios to evaluate a company's performance and financial health. These ratios can help us understand a company's profitability, liquidity, efficiency, and leverage. Consider evaluating a cricketer's batting average, strike rate, or amount of hundreds to determine their success. There are several types of ratios we look at.

"Profitability Ratios tell us how effectively a company is generating profits. The most common is the Net Profit Margin, which shows the percentage of revenue that turns into profit, and the Return on Equity, which indicates how efficiently a company uses its shareholders' equity to generate profits.

"Liquidity Ratios assess a company's ability to pay off its short-term debts. The Current Ratio and the Quick Ratio are the keys here. They compare a company's current assets to its current liabilities, giving us insight into its short-term financial health.

"Efficiency Ratios evaluate how well a company uses its assets and liabilities internally. For instance, the Asset Turnover Ratio shows how efficiently a company uses its assets to generate sales while Leverage Ratios help us understand a company's debt level. The debt-to-equity Ratio, for example, compares a company's total liabilities to its shareholder equity.

"Each of these ratios," I continued, "Provides pieces to the puzzle. Just like a cricketer's performance is judged over various conditions and against various teams, a company must be evaluated across these different parameters to understand its true financial standing."

Mr. Kapoor listened closely and nodded periodically. The analogy and precise explanation of ratio analysis significantly improved his understanding of the topic.

"In essence," I continued, "Fundamental analysis, particularly ratio analysis, helps you make more informed decisions by looking beyond the stock price. It's about understanding a company's underlying strengths and weaknesses, much like how a seasoned cricket analyst assesses a player's skill and potential."

Building on the discussion of fundamental analysis with Mr Kapoor, I decided to introduce two more crucial aspects: valuations and peer analysis.

"Mr Kapoor, alongside ratio analysis, valuations and peer analysis are key elements in fundamental analysis. These aspects help in understanding the true worth of a company and how it stands compared to its competitors.

"Let's use a cricket analogy again. Just as a cricketer's value to a team is assessed not just by individual performance but also in comparison to peers and the prevailing cricketing environment. In the stock market, understanding a company's valuation and position relative to its peers is vital.

"Valuation is about assessing what a company is truly worth. This isn't just about its current stock price but its intrinsic value. Several methods are used, such as the Price to Earnings (P/E) ratio, which compares the company's current share price to its per-share earnings. There's also the Discounted Cash Flow (DCF) analysis, which estimates the value of an investment based on its expected future cash flows, adjusted for the time value of money. These methods help determine whether a stock is overvalued or undervalued in the market.

"Peer Analysis involves comparing a company to others in the same industry or sector, similar to evaluating how a batsman performs against bowlers of the same style or in similar playing conditions. We can gauge a company's performance in the broader industry context by looking at competitors. We examine various financial metrics, market share, growth rates, and other operational parameters to understand where the company stands about its peers."

I noticed Mr. Kapoor listening closely and processing the information. "So, by conducting a thorough valuation and peer analysis, we get a comprehensive view of a company's financial health, growth prospects, and market position. It's about seeing the bigger picture, just like understanding a cricketer's worth isn't only about the runs scored in one season, but also their overall contribution to the team and their standing among contemporaries."

As the conversation continued, it became clear that these ideas gave Mr. Kapoor a new way of thinking about his investments. The comparisons to cricket, a topic he loves, seemed to connect with him, making the various concepts of stock market investing easier to understand and relate to. Then, to my surprise, Mr. Kapoor extended an invitation I hadn't anticipated. "Arjun, it's been quite an enlightening discussion. Why don't you join us for lunch?" he asked, with his tone warm and friendly.

I happily accepted the offer, and I was pleased with the change in our relationship. "Thank you, Mr. Kapoor. I'd be honoured," I said.

Meera, who had been silently listening to our chat, cheerfully said, "Dad, let's use the premium crockery set today. It's a special occasion."

Mr. Kapoor nodded in agreement, "Yes, why not? Let's make it a little special."

As Meera left the room to set the table, she looked back, winked playfully at me, and blew a quick kiss. She wanted to recognize that we were not only learning about the stock market but also getting closer to her father.

Sitting there, waiting for lunch, I couldn't help but feel a sense of acceptance. The day had turned out to be more than just a financial discussion. It was a step toward becoming a part of Meera's family. As I looked forward to lunch, I realized that these small moments of connection truly build relationships, one step at a time.

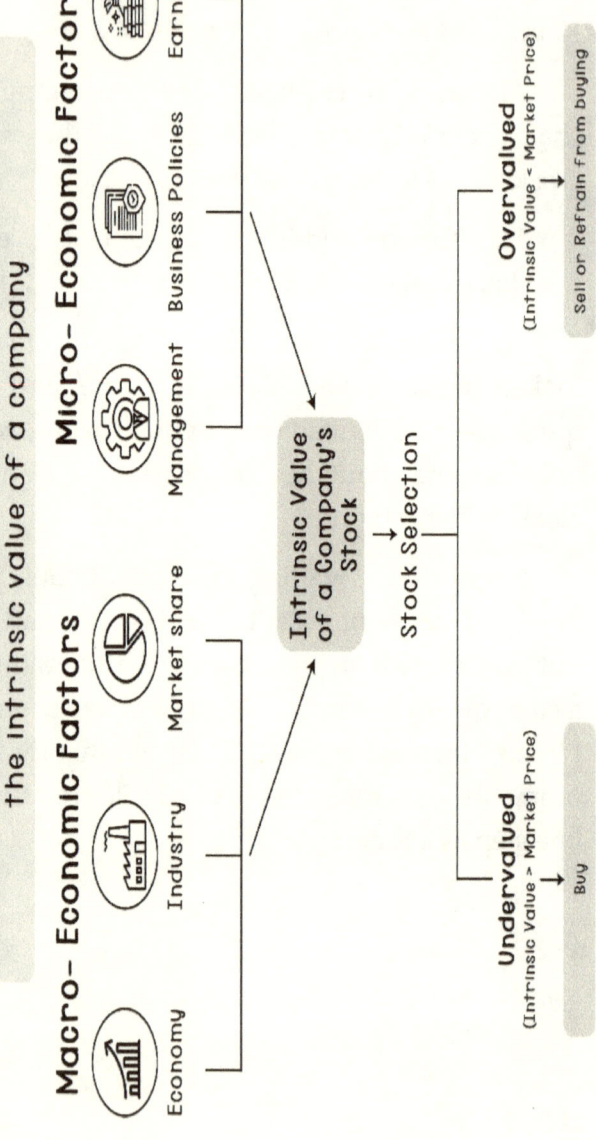

Chapter 3

The Journey Beyond Numbers, Designs, and Quantitative Easing (QE)

Meera and I stood at the bus stop early on a rainy morning. We decided to take a bus ride because Meera wanted to break away from the routine and enjoy the lovely weather, and I was ready to engage in any adventure that would strengthen our bond.

As we boarded the bus, the world outside sped up. The rain softly hit the windows, calming me. The old bus, full of stories, smoothly moved through the waking city, humming quietly in the soft rain. Meera observed everything with interest—the street vendors starting their day, children headed to school, and the city slowly coming to life under the grey skies.

We finally settled into our seats, our hands holding each other. Meera's soft voice filled the air as she shared her latest design ideas, her eyes sparkling excitedly.

She expressed her artistic vision beautifully. In return, I shared my ideas for a new financial model to help small entrepreneurs. We listened to each other intently.

Finally, as the bus trip began, the rain became more intense, water flowing down on streets and traffic increased. We reached near Lonavala in three hours. I didn't mind the delays, knowing I had the best company by my side.

As the bus moved forward, we stuck in huge traffic congestion on the expressway. Everyone on the bus appeared strained, with evident irritation. That's when the driver, with a glance through his rear-view mirror at the growing line of cars, decided that it was time for a change of plans. "Folks, we're taking a detour," he announced, turning the bus onto a less-travelled old Pune highway.

Meera looked over at me, her eyebrows raised in surprise and amusement. "Well, this is unexpected," she said, a slight smile playing at the corners of her mouth.

I nodded, watching the new scenery unfold. "It's like those sudden market turns. You think you've planned the route, and then you need a new strategy."

She laughed, leaning her head against the window. "I suppose it keeps life interesting, though. We might even discover something new this way."

"Yeah, maybe it's like exploring an unknown stock," I thought, turning to face her with a cheeky smile. "Could be risky, but there's always a chance we'll stumble on something worthwhile.

"True," Meera agreed, "And it's not like we have a meeting to rush to. We might as well enjoy the ride, right?"

"Exactly," I said, feeling the strain of the delay melting away as I looked at her. "It's all about the journey, not just the destination."

As we chatted, the bus winded through unfamiliar streets, giving us fresh views outside.

The situation sparked a thought about the surprising parallels between this unexpected journey and the global economy. I knew Mira wasn't really interested in economics like I was, but she always listened when I talked about it.

I said, "When the financial crisis happened, it was like our bus getting stuck in a big traffic jam—everything slowed down, and it seemed like we weren't going anywhere. Just like our bus driver, the Fed had to figure out how to keep things moving, even when the road ahead was blocked. So, they took a detour—that's what we call quantitative easing. They started buying bonds and putting money into the economy, like how our driver found a new route to get us out of the jam and back on track."

Meera smiled, which made me happy. I could tell she was following along. "So, are we like the passengers on this bus of economic policy?"

"Exactly," I said, grinning back. "We don't always know why the driver makes certain choices, but we trust them to get us where we need to go. The

Fed had to think about the long-term, just like our driver needs to keep the bus moving forward. The Fed also needed to keep the economy moving, ensuring it didn't stall or get stuck, even when the path ahead was uncertain."

"The goal of Quantitative Easing, or QE," I began, checking to see if Meera was interested, "Is to increase the money supply and lower interest rates by putting more money into the system. Think of it like a heavy rain filling up rivers, making it easier for everyone to get water."

Meera nodded, following my example. "So, more money means more liquidity, right?"

"Correct," I said. "When there's more liquidity, banks are encouraged to lend money to businesses and people at lower interest rates. With cheaper loans available, people are more likely to buy big things like houses or cars, and businesses can invest more in growing their companies. This whole process of increasing the money supply to boost spending and grow the economy is called Quantitative Easing."

As the rain kept falling, representing easy availability of liquidity, it spread across the countryside, filling everything with life and energy. I explained that this was similar to how the availability of money in financial markets can boost economic activity, supporting growth and prosperity.

As the bus rolled along, Meera turned to me with a thoughtful look. "Arjun, how did the stock markets do so well during tough times, like the financial crisis and COVID?"

"This 'easy liquidity'. The extra money in the system, made investors feel confident. They started buying more stocks, which pushed up prices. But there's a catch. If the central bank pulls back that money too quickly, like with something called Quantitative Tightening, or QT, it can make things shaky. When liquidity dries up, markets can drop just as quickly as they rose."

Meera frowned a bit. "So, the markets are really dependent on this money, huh?"

"Precisely," I said, squeezing her hand. "It's like the markets are on a seesaw. When there's lots of money, they go up. But if that money starts to go away, things can get bumpy."

As our bus wound its unexpected detour into the hills, we made an unplanned stop at a hillside restaurant. The environment inside the bus changed as we all looked at the remote location's higher prices, a direct consequence of its isolation and the ongoing rain.

An older man a few seats ahead turned to his companion, his voice carrying a mix of frustration and resignation. "These prices are outrageous," he said, loud enough for most of us nearby to hear. "We would've been better off sticking to the highway."

I leaned over to Meera and whispered, "The costs here have surprised everyone."

Meera nodded, eyes scanning the bus as she replied softly, "It's like when sudden inflation spikes catch investors off guard—everyone's reaction is a mix of shock and concern."

"Yeah," I agreed, watching the old man continue to voice his displeasure to anyone who would listen. "It's a bit like the economy, isn't it? When things take an unexpected turn, people's first reaction is often to wish things would go back to the familiar route, even if the new path might have its benefits."

Meera chuckled, "Exactly. Everyone prefers the route they know—even when there's no going back."

As the complaints about the restaurant prices continued, I turned to the others around us, trying to offer a different point of view. "You know, the heavy rains probably affected their deliveries, which could explain the high prices here," I added, attempting to lessen the impact of the unexpected charges.

Meera weighed in, adding another layer to the discussion, "And as we see here with the limited supply routes, when demand exceeds supply, prices rise. It's a temporary spike but perfectly demonstrates how inflation works."

I nodded, feeling the concept click for a few listeners. "And just as central banks adjust interest rates to manage economic inflation, this situation might correct itself once the weather clears and deliveries resume normal."

As we discussed the reasons behind the high prices, the mood on the bus began to change. People embraced the circumstance gently, seeing it as part of our unexpected trip.

The bus driver caught everyone's attention when he said, "I understand everyone's concerns and appreciate your patience. This detour was necessary for safety, but I'll look for a more affordable place for us to stop further down the road."

I leaned over to Meera and said in a low voice, "That helps, doesn't it? Just a little explanation and acknowledgement can make such a difference."

Meera agreed, her eyes following the driver as he navigated the bus. "It does. It's about feeling heard and knowing there's a plan. Keeps the spirits up, even when things don't go as expected."

As the bus quietly hummed along, Meera leaned in closer, her curiosity increasing. "Arjun, you mentioned that sometimes too much money in the system can cause problems. What does that mean?"

I knew this question was a bit tricky but I wanted to make it simple. "Well, think of it this way. In 2019, something similar happened. The government and the Federal Reserve were putting a lot of money into the economy to keep things running smoothly, especially by buying bonds. This made it easier and cheaper for people and businesses to borrow money—kind of like giving everyone a lot of extra pocket money."

Meera's eyes lit up as she began to understand. "So, everyone had more money to spend?"

"Yes," I continued. "But here's the thing—when there's too much money, and everyone starts spending a lot all at once, it can make prices go up really fast. That's what we call inflation. If it gets out of control like when prices skyrocket too quickly, it's called hyperinflation."

"How does central bankers keep right balance?" Meera asked, tilting her head.

"That's where it gets tricky," I replied, leaning in a bit closer. "If you keep pumping too much money into the system without pulling back at the right time, the economy could overheat. This can lead to rising prices or hyperinflation. That's why central banks eventually have to taper QE—meaning they slowly reduce how much money they're adding."

Meera seemed to be piecing it together. "But isn't it hard to just stop all of a sudden?"

"It is," I said seriously. "When the US Federal Reserve hinted at tapering QE in 2013, the markets didn't react well. Bond yields spiked, and there was a big sell-off in global markets—a situation known as the 'Taper Tantrum.' It's a delicate balancing act."

I paused for a moment. "And tapering isn't the same as Quantitative Tightening or QT. While tapering is about slowing down QE, QT is like doing the reverse—pulling back the extra money that was put into the system."

Meera raised an eyebrow, clearly intrigued. "How does QT work?"

"Quantitative Tightening, or QT," I said, "Is when the central bank starts reducing its balance sheet, either by selling bonds in the market or by letting bonds mature without reinvesting. It's like draining the excess water from a river to prevent flooding. By pulling back this extra liquidity, QT helps raise interest rates, making borrowing less attractive. When borrowing decreases, so does spending, which helps to stabilize inflation."

As the journey continued, the bus driver turned off the air conditioning, which caused some anger among the passengers. Feeling the shift in the mood, I leaned over to Meera and shared a thought.

"You see, the AC is a bit like how central bankers use Quantitative Tightening or tapering to manage liquidity in the economy," I continued, trying to make sense of the driver's decision in a way we could both relate to. "Just like the driver adjusts the AC to keep the bus comfortable, central bankers use these tools to cool down the economy when it's running too hot by gradually reducing the money supply and raising interest rates."

Meera looked thoughtful, nodding as she tied the analogy together. "So, in a way, he's adjusting liquidity based on the current conditions—similar to how a central bank might sell securities to cool down an overheated economy?"

"Yes," I replied, impressed with her quick grasp of the concept. "And just like passengers getting frustrated when the AC goes off, the traders often react negatively to economic measures like rising bond yields, especially when they start feeling the pinch because of the higher cost of funds."

Meera sighed, looking around at the other passengers. "It's all about balance, isn't it? Trying to manage the situation efficiently without making everyone uncomfortable."

"Right," I replied, strengthening the link between our current suffering and bigger economic principles. "It's a delicate act, managing not just the physical but also the economic climate. And sometimes, even well-intended actions can be a bit uncomfortable at first."

As we talked, I realised that these moments of discomfort on the bus offered a small-scale reflection of the complexities and challenges of economic management, making the journey an unexpected lesson in economics.

As the bus continued along its detoured path, the collective unease among the passengers grew palpable, making a sense of urgency. Sensing a teachable moment, I leaned closer to Meera, sharing my observations in a low voice.

"It's fascinating, isn't it? The driver is in a position much like a central bank governor right now," I observed as the driver carefully navigated the curving roads.

"How so?" Meera asked, intrigued, her eyes shifting between the driver and the restless passengers.

"Well, he's balancing safety with the passengers' demands for speed, much like how central banks manage economic stability against demands of easy economic conditions," I explained, drawing parallels to our professional knowledge of economic dynamics.

Meera grinned, loving the analogy. "It's a real-time lesson in economic policy and public sentiment, right? Observing how he handles this situation gives us a small-scale reflection of economic policy making."

"Definitely," I replied, overseeing the driver manage every turn. "It's about navigating carefully, not just the roads but also the economic landscape."

"See, just like our bus driver navigating these turns; central banks have to be careful about when and how they adjust their policies," I said, gesturing slightly towards the driver as he concentrated on the road.

Meera listened intently, her eyes reflecting understanding. "And if they're too slow, the economy might sink into a downturn, similar to how being overly cautious could make us miss our destination or get stuck," she added, expanding on the metaphor.

"Exactly," I nodded, pleased with her quick grasp of the comparison. "It's all about timing and measure. Too much or too little adjustment can lead to problems, just like on our current journey."

Meera smiled, her gaze returning to the road ahead. "It puts into perspective the delicate balance they must maintain to keep everything running smoothly."

As the bus rolled forward, our conversation deepened, weaving together observations from the day into one that highlighted our personal growth and evolving understanding of the world around us. Though unexpected, this bus ride enriched our perspectives. It strengthened our bond, a testament to the enduring power of shared experiences and learned truths.

What Is Quantitative Easing (QE)?

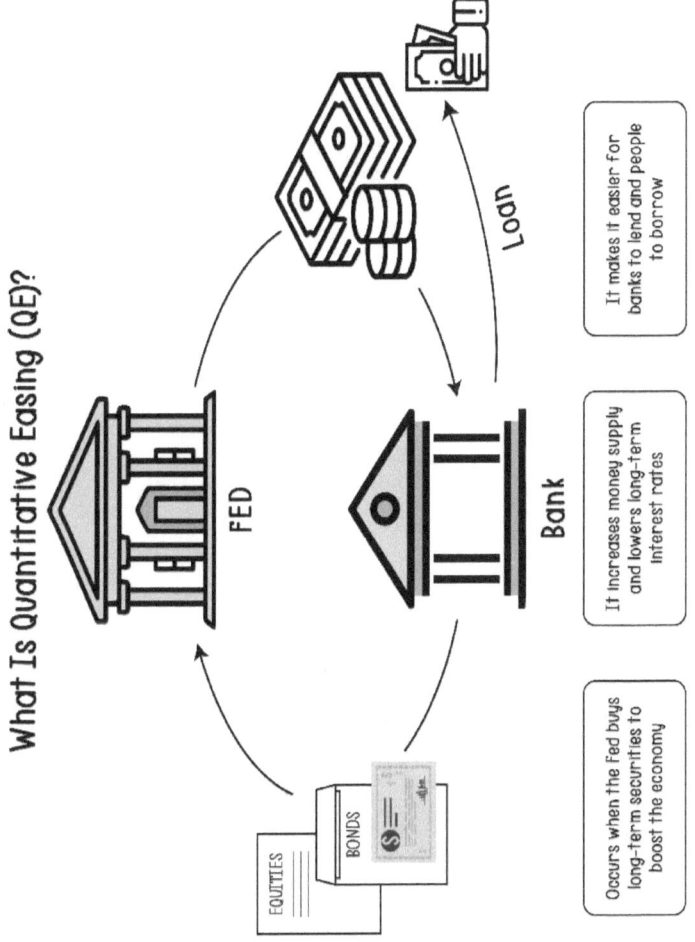

Chapter 4

Lessons from the Heart - Navigating Behavioral Finance through Kabir's Tale

Meera and I sat across from each other in the relaxing atmosphere of a local Starbucks. The aroma of coffee beans and the soft buzz of conversations created a warm and comforting ambiance. We chose this spot to reflect on the day's events and contemplate the future, a rare moment of stillness in our otherwise busy lives.

As we ordered coffee, my phone, lying on the table, vibrated with an incoming call. The screen displayed my brother Rahul's name; an unexpected call at this time. With a smile on my face, I excused myself to respond, "Arjun, it`s Rahul", my brother's voice came through, tinged with concern. "I got a call from Kabir's school. He hasn't been attending classes for a week, and they tried contacting me, but I missed the calls. I'm travelling to Singapore for work and can't handle this from here. Can you look into the situation for me?"

I felt a chill despite the warmth of the café. Kabir, a happy and active four-year-old nephew who loved the school, missed school for a week. How had the situation escalated to this point without Rahul's intervention? A terrible anxiety started to eat at me.

"Don't worry, Rahul. I'll look into it right away," I reassured him, attempting to address his concern. I knew my brother Rahul was miles away in

Singapore and was unable to address the matter directly.

Meera's worried eyes greeted mine as I hung up the phone. "What's wrong, Arjun? Is everything okay with Kabir?" she asked, her voice low, acutely aware of the seriousness of the situation.

I relayed the conversation to Meera. We spent the rest of our coffee break in quiet, buried in thought and concern for Kabir.

We decided to leave immediately, abandoning the coffees, which were now cold and forgotten. The drive to Rahul's house was tense. Our minds were filled with anxiety about Kabir, so the streets we passed felt both familiar and yet distant.

When we got to the house, everything was quiet. The lively laughter and banter that usually filled the room was noticeably absent. After a few persistent knocks, the door opened to reveal my sister-in-law's stressed and worried expression.

I sat next to Kabir in his cozy bedroom, surrounded by his colorful toys and drawings on the walls. It was unusually quiet.

Kabir looked at me with his innocent eyes. "Kabir," I said gently but firmly, "Your school called today. They were worried because you haven't been to school for a week. Is everything okay?"

Kabir's brows wrinkled in confusion. His little hand reached out to grab a nearby stuffed animal, a source of comfort in the growing tension. After hesitating, he looked up at me with his voice carrying a surprising confidence. "But, I've been going to school every day, uncle Arjun," he stated emphatically.

The confidence in Kabir's voice surprised me. It felt reassuring, yet it just increased the uncertainty. Where did the misunderstanding come from, if Kabir thought he was going to school regularly?

Sensing the need to clarify the situation further, I decided to dig deeper. "Do you go to your classroom every day? Are you with your friends and teacher?" I asked, attempting to put together the child's concept of "going to school".

Kabir nodded enthusiastically. "Yes! I go to school. I sit with my best friend Uncle Arjun," Kabir said, clutching his toy animal close.

"I'm in a new class, and Miss Anu is the new teacher."

"What section have you been sitting in?" I asked.

Kabir said, "Prep II C."

I then noticed that his actual class was Prep II A, as stated on his ID card, which explained everything.

I asked, "Why have you been sitting in the wrong class?"

He responded, "I wanted to sit with my best friend Sarthak."

Kabir further clarified, "*Naye class main mera naam Kabir Mishra ho gaya hai.*" (My name has changed to Kabir Mishra in the new class). Kabir was even marking attendance under his new identity in this new classroom.

We laughed out loud at his remark, which clarified the issue and added a hint of comedy. Piecing together the story from Kabir's innocent admission, I couldn't help but be impressed by the simplicity with which children navigate their world. When faced with a new environment and establishing new acquaintances, Kabir found a unique solution. He adopted the name 'Kabir Mishra', which was wrongly allocated to him because he was in the incorrect class, and this helped him blend in smoothly.

The mix-up with the attendance now made perfect sense. Kabir went to school daily but under the name "Kabir Mishra." This identity switch, which resulted from being mistakenly placed in the wrong class, had caused confusion. The school administration couldn't find him in the attendance records because they were looking for Kabir in the A section, not realizing he was present all along as "Kabir Mishra" in the C section. This explained why they thought he was missing, even though he had been there daily.

With a plan in mind, I sat down with Kabir. I explained why he needed to use his real name. I reassured him that making new friends, while scary at first, was a part of growing up. I promised to accompany him to school to sort out the confusion.

I could see his concern, so I tried to make him feel better. "I'll be there with you the whole time," I promised. "We'll talk to your teacher and explain everything. And I'll help you meet your new classmates. You're not alone in this."

Kabir seemed to relax a bit. "Okay," he said quietly. I hugged him, knowing that we'd get through this together.

The next day, we accompanied Kabir to school, a small adventure filled with excitement and nervous anticipation for the little boy. Together, we met with the teachers, explained the misunderstanding, and reintroduced Kabir to his class with his correct name.

The teachers, understanding and supportive, facilitated the process, ensuring Kabir felt comfortable and welcomed in his skin.

This part of Kabir's early life was not just a mix-up; it was a self – discovery lesson, learning how to deal with the complexities of social interactions, and finding one's place in a new environment. For Meera and me, it reminded us of the never-ending surprises and important lessons found in the simplicity of a child's world, as well as the happiness of supporting them through their many adventures. It reminded Meera and me of the innocence of a child's world, with their never-ending surprises in their simplicities. And the joy ride of supporting their many adventures.

Kabir's tale is an excellent example of how cognitive biases, particularly confirmation bias, shape our decisions and perceptions, even outside the scope of finance and investing.

Confirmation Bias

Kabir's subconscious choice to believe he was in the right class despite the mix-up, as well as his reaction to attendance calls, demonstrate how confirmation bi

as can manifest. He sought comfort and confirmation in his existing belief—the desire to stay with his friend—leading him to adopt a new identity.

His actions were motivated by the deep-seated human tendency to seek out and interpret information in a way that confirms our preconceptions.

The Teacher's Oversight

In the daily roll calls, the instructor anticipated hearing a "Present!" This demonstrates how confirmation bias may affect group dynamics and an individual's experiences.

This expectation, combined with the belief that students were where they belonged, led to the oversight of Kabir's identity swap. It's a compelling demonstration of how seeking confirmation can sometimes blind us to discrepancies right in front of our eyes.

Implications in Investing

Paralleling Kabir's incident to the world of investing, confirmation bias can lead investors to filter out market signals or research that contradicts their investment thesis.

Just as Kabir and his teacher clung to their initial beliefs for comfort and routine, investors might ignore warning signs or alternative views, focusing only on information that supports their decisions. This selective information processing can lead to missed opportunities or overlooked risks, affecting overall health and diversity of an investment portfolio.

Mitigating Confirmation Bias

Recognizing and mitigating confirmation bias involves actively seeking out and considering information and viewpoints that challenge our current beliefs. It's about broadening our informational horizon and being open to adjustment and change.

Just as a reflective moment might have led Kabir or his teacher to question the classroom mix-up sooner, investors benefit from periodically stepping back and critically assessing their investment strategies against a broader spectrum of information.

Kabir's unintended lessons in cognitive bias stresses the importance of awareness and critical thinking, both in the innocence of a classroom setting and the complexity of financial markets.

Recognizing the influence of confirmation bias allows individuals to make more informed, rational decisions, whether in friendships, teaching, or investing.

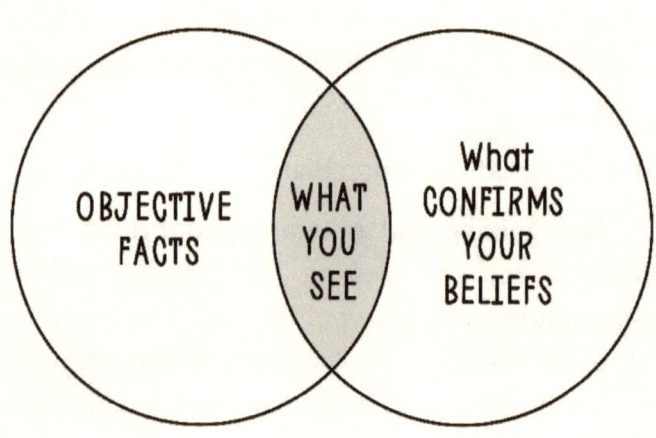

Information Bias

Information bias happens when someone already has enough information to make a decision but keeps looking for more, which can lead to confusion and make it harder to choose what to do. This was clear in how the teacher and the school handled Kabir's attendance. They had enough information to question the mix-up but didn't look deeper because they were focused on the fact that a student named Kabir was present.

In the financial aspect, this bias plays out when investors gather excessive data beyond what is necessary to decide. For example, an investor might spend hours analyzing every possible report on a company or economic forecasts, trying to predict stock movements. While being informed is crucial, there comes a point where additional information does not contribute to a better decision-making process. Instead, it may lead to analysis paralysis, where the investor becomes so bogged down in data that making a decision becomes overwhelmingly complicated, or they stick to their initial decision without considering simpler, more important pieces of information.

This parallels the school's situation with Kabir, where the simple fact that should have triggered a closer look — the specific identity of the attending Kabir — was glossed over in favour of the reassurance that a student named Kabir was present. Similarly, investors might overlook fundamental indicators of a stock's potential, such as the company's earnings or the market's overall direction, in favour of complex analyses or speculative data.

When it comes to investing, it's easy to get affected by all the information out there. But if you can tune out the unnecessary chatter and focus on what really matters, you're more likely to avoid mistakes and make smarter, well-informed decisions.

Loss Aversion/Endowment Effect –

Kabir's reluctance to leave his friend's side and join the correct class highlights loss aversion and the endowment effect. He overvalued the existing relationship (what he "owned"), fearing the loss of this connection more than the potential gain from making new friends. Investors often exhibit similar behaviour, holding onto losing stocks due to an emotional attachment or the fear of realizing a loss despite rational reasons to sell.

Kabir's story beautifully demonstrates the psychological phenomena of loss aversion and the endowment effect. His attachment to his friend and his fear of losing that close connection overshadowed the potential benefits of meeting new peers and experiencing new interactions in the correct class. This behaviour reflects a natural human tendency to weigh potential losses more heavily than equivalent gains, a principle known as loss aversion. The endowment effect complements this by describing how individuals ascribe more value to things merely because they own them, in this case, Kabir's existing friendship.

In investing, these biases manifest when individuals hold onto underperforming assets. The reluctance to sell such assets often stems from an emotional attachment or the sunk cost fallacy—the belief that more can be recouped by holding onto them longer, even when evidence suggests otherwise. Like Kabir, investors might fear the "loss" associated with selling a stock at a lower price than they purchased it, even if that decision would prevent further losses or free up capital for more promising investments.

This behaviour can lead to an unbalanced portfolio dominated by underperforming assets, hindering overall investment growth. Recognizing and overcoming loss aversion and the endowment effect requires a shift in perspective. For Kabir, this might mean focusing on the new friendships and learning opportunities awaiting him in his class. For investors, it involves evaluating assets based on current and future value rather than past costs or emotional attachments.

Strategies to combat these biases include setting predetermined criteria for selling assets, such as a specific loss threshold or time frame for reevaluation, and diversifying investments to minimize the impact of any single loss. Additionally, seeking the perspective of an unbiased third party can provide objective insights that counterbalance personal biases.

By understanding and addressing loss aversion and the endowment effect, individuals can make more rational decisions, whether navigating social dynamics in a school setting or managing a portfolio in the financial markets. Kabir's story reminds us that while emotional attachments are a powerful aspect of human psychology, they can cloud judgment and make it harder to see and take advantage of good opportunities and positive changes.

Incentive-Caused Bias

The incentive-caused bias in Kabir's scenario is subtle but present in his motivation to maintain his comfort zone, illustrating how incentives can skew actions and perceptions. Similarly, investors may be swayed by short-term gains or bonuses, potentially leading to decisions not aligned with long-term objectives.

In Kabir's narrative, the incentive to stay within his comfort zone — maintaining proximity to his friend — clearly showcases incentive-caused bias. This bias demonstrates how certain rewards or incentives can influence our actions, sometimes leading us away from more rational or beneficial paths.

For Kabir, the immediate relief of avoiding the stress of making new friends and adjusting to a new environment seemed more important than the long-term benefit of being in the right class where his education needs would be better met.

Similarly, in the financial world, investors often face what's known as incentive-caused bias. The temptation of quick profits or attractive bonuses from certain investments can distract them from staying focused on their long-term financial goals.An investor might be tempted to invest in a high-risk stock promising rapid returns rather than adhering to a well-thought-out, diversified investment plan designed for steady, long-term growth. Here, the immediate incentive (potential for quick gain) biases the investor's decision-making process, overshadowing the importance of strategy and long-term planning.

This bias can be particularly detrimental when it leads to actions misaligned with an individual's or organization's long-term objectives. For example, a company might focus on strategies that boost short-term stock prices at the expense of long-term sustainability, influenced by the incentive of immediate market performance or bonuses tied to stock prices.

Combatting incentive-caused bias requires a conscious effort to recognize the underlying incentives driving our decisions and to question whether they align with our broader goals and values.

For investors, this might mean implementing a rigorous evaluation process that scrutinizes potential investments beyond their immediate appeal, considering their fit within the broader investment strategy. It also involves being mindful of how external incentives, such as tax implications or broker commissions, might influence investment choices.

For Kabir, overcoming the bias might involve understanding the value of being in the right classroom setting for his long-term educational growth and recognizing that making new friends is a part of his developmental process.

Similarly, investors must look beyond the immediate facinationj of potential gains, carefully weighing decisions against their long-term financial health and objectives.

In both cases, the key lies in awareness and a disciplined approach to decision-making. This ensures that actions are driven by well-considered, long-term benefits rather than immediate incentives. By doing so, one can navigate the complexities of social and financial environments more effectively, making choices aligned with broader goals and lasting benefits.

Oversimplification Tendency

Kabir's solution to his problem was to simply assume a new identity, an oversimplification of a more complex issue. This mirrors investors' tendencies to rely on simplified heuristics or trends without considering the underlying complexities of financial instruments or market conditions.

In the captivating drama of Kabir's school life, a scene unfolds that would captivate any audience with its simplicity and childlike innocence. Confronted with the social complexities is of a new classroom, Kabir chooses a straightforward and imaginative path.

Kabir's desire for comfort and familiarity causes him to miss out on the valuable experiences and lessons that come with interacting with new environments and people. Although adopting a new identity may help reduce his loneliness in the short term, it does not address the important processes of personal growth and adaptation.

Some investors in financial markets make a mistake similar to Kabir's, but in a different way. Instead of doing thorough research, they take shortcuts, like trading based on WhatsApp tips without checking the facts. This oversimplification can hurt their long-term wealth creation.

The tendency to oversimplify can lead investors to go off track , similar to Kabir in his makeshift identity. They rely on quick answers by following broad trends or using mental shortcuts, trying to understand the market's complicated signals.

These investors follow catchy headlines or the latest trends without really understanding how the market works, how individual stocks perform, or what the economy is doing. While this simple approach might seem easier, it risks missing the important details of the market, leading to decisions that might not last or handle changes well over time.

Kabir's story and an investor's journey are quite similar, showing how both kids and experienced investors can sometimes oversimplify things and miss important details in their situations. For Kabir, adopting a new identity might miss the invaluable lessons in resilience, empathy, and friendship that come from facing new challenges head-on. For investors, relying on simplification could mean missed opportunities for growth, diversification, and a deeper understanding of their investments.

The oversimplification we see in both a child's school life and in financial markets reminds us that there is so much to learn from the complexity around us. It shows us how important it is to accept and understand this complexity with an open heart and mind.

Bandwagon Effect (or Herd Mentality)

Even though it doesn't apply directly to Kabir's decision, the bandwagon effect is common in classrooms and playgrounds, where kids follow popular trends. In financial markets, this happens when investors join in on trends without doing proper research, often because they are afraid of missing out (FOMO).

In the exciting world of childhood, where the playground is like a stage and the latest craze is the main attraction, kids often get caught up in the excitement, just like actors in a big show. This bandwagon effect happens when kids' individual interests turn into a group obsession, with everyone talking about the newest game, toy, or challenge.

Kabir understands the pull of popular trends, and he is no stranger to it. In this world, adopting what's popular isn't just about fitting in; it's about not being left behind.

In financial markets, many investors follow the crowd without doing their own research. They may be drawn to popular stocks or assets because of rising prices and media attention, rather than analyzing the investment's fundamentals. While offering the comfort of the company on the journey, this herd mentality can lead to inflated asset bubbles and, ultimately, dramatic corrections when the trend reverses.

For investors, this could lead to decisions that don't match their financial goals or comfort with risk, as they get caught up in the excitement of market trends. Social cues have a powerful influence on our actions and decisions, sometimes causing us to follow trends without considering our own preferences. This can lead investors to make choices that don't align with their financial goals and risk tolerance. They may get caught up in market trends and forget to do their due diligence.

BANDWAGON EFFECT

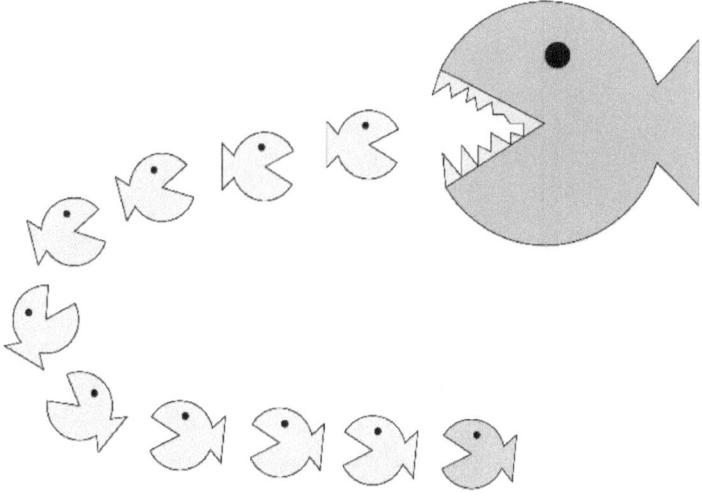

Recognizing the bandwagon effect means taking a moment to step back from following the crowd and think about your own values, preferences, and goals. Whether you're choosing a game to play or making an investment, it's important to listen to your own thoughts instead of just going along with everyone else. This skill can help you make more authentic choices, whether it's on the playground or in the market.

Restraint Bias

Kabir's story teaches us about the concept of restraint bias, which occurs when someone believes they have more self-control or can manage things better than they actually can. In his eagerness and innocence, Kabir thought he could solve his problem on his own without asking for help, displaying restraint bias. He didn't consider the potential confusion his actions might cause. This tendency to believe we can handle difficult situations on our own, even when we might need help, is a common challenge people face.

Kabir's experience can be applied to other areas, such as investing in the stock market. Similar to Kabir, investors may overestimate their ability to handle tough market conditions. When the market is doing well, they feel confident and believe they can stay composed during market fluctuations. However, when times get tough, like during a market downturn, their confidence can quickly diminish, leading to impulsive decisions that may not be in their best interest.

This restraint bias can be particularly risky while investing, as it can lead investors to make decisions that go against their long-term goals. For instance, during a market downturn, investors may panic and sell their stocks despite intending to hold them for the long term. Alternatively, they might invest too much in a rising market without considering the need to diversify their investments or manage risks.

Kabir's story and t the theory of investing emphasizes on the importance of recognizing our limitations. Just as Kabir needed to acknowledge his need for help, investors need to recognize how their emotions can lead to poor decisions during challenging market conditions.

Overcoming restraint bias involves acknowledging our limitations and being willing to seek help when necessary. For Kabir, this could mean seeking advice from teachers or family members to understand the value of seeking new experiences. For investors, it might involve establishing guidelines for decision-making in advance or consulting financial advisors to align their actions with their long-term objectives.

Both cases highlight the need for growth and learning in overcoming restraint bias. It's about striking a balance between confidence and caution. By recognizing when we need help and being open to guidance, we can n negotiate life's challenges more successfully, whether it's a child adjusting to school or an investor managing their finances in a complex market environment.

Kabir's story and the idea of investing serve as a reminder that it's acceptable to seek help and advice when needed. Doing so can lead to better decision-making and a brighter future, whether in the classroom or in the scope of finance.

Neglect of Probability

Kabir believed he could get away with pretending to be someone else without getting caught. However, this is an example of "neglect of probability", where someone disregards the likelihood of something happening because they are too focused on their desires. In the context of investing, this is similar to when individuals pursue high rewards without considering the associated risks.

In Kabir's school life, which was filled with innocence and imagination, he made an error by not considering potential negative outcomes. He adopted a new identity, thinking it would help him better fit in, without contemplating the possibility of being discovered. Kabir's mind was so preoccupied with the benefits of attending school in PREP I C (wrong class) else that he didn't take into account the likelihood of being caught and the potential consequences.

This story illustrates how we sometimes overlook the probability of things not going according to plan. For Kabir, the thrill of his new identity caused him to overlook the risks, potentially leading to confusion or trouble in the future. Similarly, in investing, people often overlook risks when they are overly fixated on potential gains, which can result in problems later on.

This same kind of thinking, called "cognitive bias", can also happen when people invest money. Investors are often tempted by the idea of making a lot of money quickly, just like Kabir was excited about his new identity. But when they focus too much on the big rewards, they can forget about the risks involved. They might ignore warning signs or important facts that suggest they could lose money, and instead, they only think about how much they could gain.

This way of thinking can lead investors to take on investments that are too risky. They might put all their money into one thing, instead of spreading it out across different investments, which would be safer. If things don't go as planned, they could lose a lot of money because they didn't consider the chances of things going wrong. Just like Kabir didn't think about the possibility of getting caught, investors might not think about the possibility of losing money, which can cause big problems if the situation changes suddenly.

Overcoming the neglect of probability is crucial for making smarter decisions, whether in the world of investing or in everyday life. For investors, it's not just about chasing big rewards; it's about being aware of the risks that come with them. By thinking about what could go wrong, using solid research, diversifying investments, setting clear goals, and seeking advice from experts, investors can make more balanced and thoughtful choices.

Anchoring Bias

In Kabir's story, anchoring bias is seen in the initial mistake of being called the wrong name, which influenced everyone's actions and perceptions afterwards. In investing, this bias occurs when the first piece of information heavily impacts all future decisions, like the initial price of a stock shaping its perceived value regardless of market changes.

In Kabir's early adventures, a simple mistake led to a series of events that can help us understand anchoring bias. When the teacher accidentally called him Kabir Mishra, it started a chain of events. This small error became the focus for Kabir, his teacher, and his classmates, shaping their interactions and views without them realizing it. Kabir accepted this new name, and his teacher associated him with it, showing how a single piece of information can influence actions and beliefs. This mistake wasn't just a small oversight but a starting point that made everyone think and act in a certain way.

In the area of financial markets, anchoring bias plays a significant role in shaping investor behavior.

This bias occurs when investors become fixated on the initial price at which they encounter a stock, which then influences all subsequent perceptions of the stock's value. This can lead to holding onto a declining stock in the hope that it will rebound to its initial price or hesitating to invest in a rising stock because it was once available at a lower cost. Just as the initial calling of "Kabir Mishra" became the reference point around which Kabir's school life revolved, the initial price of a stock can become the reference point around which investors frame their buying and selling decisions, often disregarding new information that should logically adjust their valuation.

ANCHORING EFFECT

The anchoring bias reveals the powerful influence of first impressions and initial data points in colouring our decisions and perceptions over time. For Kabir, the consequences were relatively benign, entailing a mix-up in identity that could be rectified with explanations and adjustments. However, for investors, the stakes are significantly higher. Anchoring to an initial price without accounting for market dynamics, company performance, and other relevant factors can lead to missed opportunities and substantial financial losses.

Recognizing and mitigating anchoring bias requires a conscious effort to detach from initial data points and continuously reevaluate decisions in light of new information.

For Kabir, it meant understanding and accepting his true identity, regardless of the name first called. For investors, it involves regularly reviewing investment decisions based on the latest market data and financial analyses, ensuring that actions are guided by current realities rather than anchored to past perceptions. This adaptive approach, both in navigating the complexities of childhood and the intricacies of investing, is critical to making informed, rational decisions free from the disproportionate influence of initial anchors.

As I explained the concept of cognitive biases to Meera, we both realized that we were sitting in a small café near Kabir's school. It had been a day filled with discoveries as we uncovered what had been happening during Kabir's school days. As I sat there, I felt very calmed. Our conversation and shared learning not only made me feel better, but also brought Meera and me closer. We sat quietly, thankful for the journey we had shared, the challenges we had gone through together, and the comfort of being together.

In the gentle light, I held Meera's hand. Our fingers naturally came together, as if they belonged as one I felt the connection we had built through all the challenges we faced together. I moved closer and quietly thanked Meera, showing my appreciation and love. She smiled warmly, her eyes reflecting emotions that didn't need words.

"I love you, Arjun," she whispered, her voice filled with sincerity and warmth.

I approached Meera, and we ended up with our faces very close to each other. I kissed her gently, feeling the warmth of her breath. Our kiss was full of love, closing on our emotional bond. It was a moment where everything else faded away. We felt connected in a way that didn't need words. When we pulled away, we rested our foreheads together and with our eyes closed. Then, Meera opened her eyes, smiled at me. The love and peace we found in each other resonating on to us.

Chapter 5

Yields of Affection: Navigating the Bonds of Love and Finance

Meera and I had had a busy month, but our love continued to grow. Despite our demanding jobs, we found new ways to amplify our relationship. During one of our evening calls, Meera was excited to tell me about a big order she had received. I could feel her happiness even over the phone.

"Arjun, you won't believe it. We just landed our biggest order yet! It was both thrilling and terrifying," she said, her voice a mix of excitement and stress.

"I can only imagine," I replied, anticipated. "Your dedication is remarkable, Meera. But please tell me you weren't just living off coffee and adrenaline."

"Guilty as charged!" she admitted with a slight laugh, but then her tone grew more serious. "But seriously, it's testing my every limit. I'm learning so much, yet it feels like I'm walking a tightrope. Every decision feels so important."

"I wish I could see you in action," I said, my voice filled with admiration. "You've got this incredible strength, Meera."

"I know," she sighed, "I just... don't want to disappoint anyone. My team is counting on me, and now there's this added expectation from our families."

"We'll handle this challenge like we always do," I told her. "We'll plan your order and show our families how well we work together."

"This order is overwhelming," she confessed. "It could put us on the map, but it requires perfection, especially with everything else happening..."

"Listen, Meera," I said, "Your talent got you here, not luck. You will handle this order perfectly. And regarding us, we will handle the family pressure together."

"You're right," she said, smiling, clearly reassured. "When did you become the wise one?"

"Probably around the same time you decided to take on the fashion world by storm," I joked.

She hesitated for a moment before adding, "Actually, there's something else... My grandfather's in town. He arrived unexpectedly last night."

"Oh, wow! I didn't know he was visiting. How's that going?" I asked, surprised.

"It's... complicated," she admitted. "He is old-school, you know? Very traditional. And he has a lot of opinions about how I was running the business and my personal life, too."

"That sounds tough," I said understandingly. "I can only imagine the pressure. How are you holding up?"

"It is somewhat scary," she said softly. "I respect him a lot, but it is hard when he questions the choices I am so sure about, like us. He doesn't know we are together, and I'm unsure of how he'll take it."

"I understand," I said softly. "Family expectations can be tough, especially when they come from a different time. Have you thought about how you want to deal with it?"

"I've been thinking about it," she said. "I want him to see that the world has changed and that I can make my own decisions. And those decisions are stronger because you're in my life."

"That's a good approach, Meera," I told her. "Maybe it's about finding the right moment, or easing him into the idea. Either way, it sounds good."

"Thanks, Arjun. It means a lot knowing you are here. Hopefully, he'll see that our love and respect for each other is mutual."

"He will," I assured her. "We'll show it. And hey, if there is any way I can help, even if it is just being there when you talk to him, say the word."

"There's more to his visit," she continued with a note of worry creeping into her voice. "It wasn't just about checking in on me. He has been facing some issues with his investments in debt funds. It seems he isn't making the returns he expected, and it has got him worried."

"Has he spoken to you about what has been happening with those investments?" I asked, concerned.

"A bit," she replied. "He is quite guarded about it, but I could tell it is stressing him out. Seeing his money not work as he anticipated is unsettling."

"I understand," I said, nodding. "And it isn't just about the money. It is the sense of security that has become disturbed. But you know, Meera, I've been keeping an eye on the markets and reading up on debt funds lately. Maybe I could help him review his portfolio and see if there are any adjustments to be made."

"Will you?" she asked, her voice filled with gratitude. "That would mean the world to him—and to me."

"Of course," I said, smiling. "I'd be glad to help. It might also be a good opportunity for me to talk to him and bridge the gap on a different front. We can look at his investments together, try to understand his goals, and maybe realign his portfolio accordingly."

"That is nice, Arjun," she said warmly. "I think he'd appreciate it."

"That's the plan," I said confidently. "It will give me a chance to bond with him better."

"I love that idea," she said, sounding more hopeful. "It might just make him see it all a bit differently, including how he sees us. I'll talk to him about it, and set up a time for you two to sit down together."

"Perfect," I said. "We'll approach this carefully while also making it a learning opportunity for all of us. And remember, no matter what, we are in this together."

"Thank you, Arjun," she said softly, and I could hear the relief in her voice.

When I arrived at Meera's house that weekend, I felt more relaxed than usual. Usually, I'd be a bit nervous, but this time, I was just calm. Everything was familiar as I stepped through the door. Instead of feeling tense, I was greeted with a warm, comfortable atmosphere. It was a nice change from what I usually expected.

I spent some time chatting with Meera's father about stocks, bonds, and mutual funds, diving into market projections. We had a great conversation covering complex financial topics and I shared the joy of sharing knowledge with someone genuinely interested.

As the weekend's informal investment seminar came to a close, we got to the matter we were more concerned about: Meera's grandfather and the difficulty of his investments.

Known affectionately as 'Daadu' within the family, Meera's grandfather was a figure who commanded respect not just for his age but for the life he had lived and the wisdom he had accumulated. Daadu was a man of another era, his demeanour and attire a tribute to his roots and the values he held dear. He dressed with an uncommon elegance in today's world, favouring crisp, hand-stitched kurtas over the casual attire of the younger generation. His spectacles, always perched on the bridge of his nose, had thin gold rims that gleamed in the light, complementing the streaks of silver in his neatly combed hair. A walking stick, more a symbol of his years than a necessity, often accompanied him, its handle carved from the finest wood, telling stories of the past.

His presence in the room was like a gentle but firm reminder of the traditions and the disciplined way of life that he lived. Yet, beneath this mask of strictness, Daadu had a curiosity and a keen intellect that had not dulled with age. The recent challenges with his investments were not a result of a lack of knowledge but rather the result of a swiftly changing market, causing his previously successful strategies to struggle.

Meera approached the topic with Daadu with apprehension and resolve. We found him in his favourite armchair, reading a hindi newspaper. The room, filled with old photos and artefacts, felt like the right place to have this important conversation.

"Daadu," Meera began, "We've been talking about investments today, and Arjun has some thoughts on your portfolio. Would you mind if we discussed it?"

Daadu glanced at Meera then at me, and smiled. "I guess I've been learning new things from the market," he chuckled. "What do you have in mind, young man?"

When I noticed that Daadu was receptive to talking, I approached him. Instead of using complex financial terms, I spoke plainly and clearly because I wanted to be helpful.

"Young man," Daadu began, speaking with the wisdom of his years, "I appreciate your insights. But there's an issue that's been bothering me - my investments in debt funds. It seems the market's behaviour has become more unpredictable." I leaned in, noticing that Daadu's tone had changed. I locked in in the conversation. Meera sat close by, listening, hoping to get what we wanted to from it all.

Daadu was lost in thought as he traced the patterns on his walking stick. He had always been cautious with his investments, choosing the stable and predictable returns of debt funds. It wasn't just the financial impact that troubled him; it was the realization that the world he knew, the rules he had played by, were changing faster than he could adapt. His investments, which used to give him pride and security, now felt like they were mocking him, questioning all his years of experience.

I nodded, understanding the depth of Daadu's dilemma. "Debt funds, while generally more stable, are not immune to market dynamics," I explained, choosing my words carefully. "Interest rate movements, credit risk, and market sentiment can all impact returns. However, there are strategies we can explore to mitigate these risks and realign your portfolio to match your risk tolerance and financial goals."

I decided to talk about a problem that had caused Daadu's investments in debt funds to yield low to negative returns. The culprit, as identified, was the recent hikes in the repo rate by the central bank, a scenario that had inversely affected the performance of Daadu's chosen debt instruments.

Seeing that it was important to make things clear, I explained how debt funds work and how their value fluctuates in response to changes in interest rates. I wanted Daadu to understand the fundamental relationship between prices and yields.

"Daadu," I began, speaking respectfully but clearly, "Debt funds invest in fixed-income securities. These could be government bonds, corporate bonds, or other debt instruments. Each of these securities has a coupon rate, which is the fixed interest rate being paid on these bonds." I paused to ensure that Daadu was following and saw that he was listening closely.

"Understanding your fund's performance depends on the relationship between yield movements in the economy, particularly in response to repo rate adjustments and the bond prices in your fund's portfolio. This relationship is inversely proportional." Daadu nodded, letting me know to continue.

"When the central bank raises the repo rate, newly issued bonds come with higher interest rates, making them more appealing to investors due to their better returns. As a result, existing bonds in your portfolio with lower interest rates become less attractive. Additionally, investors' demand for the higher interest rate on these bonds also causes their market price to decline."

I observed Daadu, ensuring the concept was digesting well before continuing.

"Here's where the price-yield relationship comes into play. As the price of these bonds drops, their yield—an indicator of the return investors can expect—increases, but not in a way that benefits current holders. For an investor holding onto these bonds, this situation translates to temporary losses, reflecting the low to negative returns you've experienced."

Meera interjected, offering Daadu a warm, supportive glance. "So, it's not about the quality of your investments but the market's reaction to external economic policies."

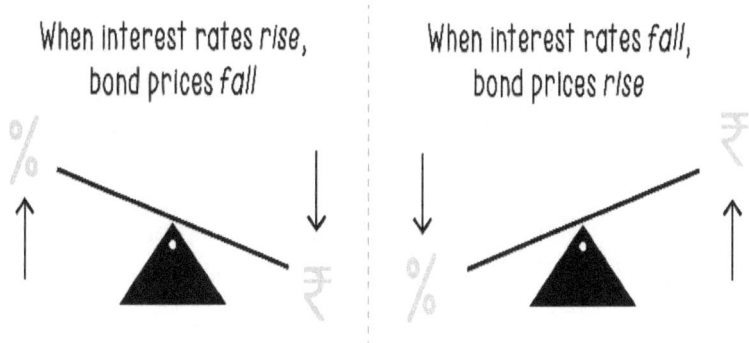

"Exactly," I said, nodding in agreement. "Your debt funds are simply responding to the current economic shifts. But keep in mind, Daadu, these changes are typically short-lived. As the bonds near their maturity date, their value tends to revert to what you initially invested, barring any defaults."

"Arjun, my boy," Daadu interrupted, his tone reflecting both an eager learner and the sage wisdom of his years. "Before we continue, can you explain the difference between yield and coupon? These terms come up often in our conversations, but I find the distinction somewhat unclear."

When Daadu showed a keen interest in understanding financial terms, I was glad to explain. "Sure, Daadu," I began, trying to simplify it. "The coupon rate of a bond is simply the interest rate that the issuer pays every year based on the bond's face value. It's determined when the bond is issued and remains unchanged. For example, if you have a bond worth Rs. 1000 with a 5% coupon rate, you'll receive Rs. 50 each year until the bond matures."

Daadu nodded, the concept of the coupon rate aligning with his understanding of how bonds traditionally worked, offering a fixed income over their tenure.

I continued, "The coupon rate of a bond remains fixed, while its yield changes with the market. For example, if a bond's market price drops from Rs. 1000 to Rs. 900, and the annual interest remains at Rs. 50, the yield increases. This is because the same income is received from a lower investment. Consequently, yield is a good indicator of the bond's current value and attractiveness compared to other investments.

Daadu quickly understood and explained, "The coupon has stayed the same since the bond started. But the yield changes with the market, showing how the bond is doing now."

YIELD VS COUPON

The yield of the bond is the rate of return on the bond	Coupon rate of the bond is rate of interest that the bond pays
Yield changes when market changes	Coupon remains same for entire duration of the bond

"Exactly," I nodded in agreement. "This is why investors closely monitor the yield. It not only indicates the income they can expect but also provides insight into the bond's market value and the risks associated with changes in interest rates."

"Daddu, there's another important aspect that can help you effectively manage your investments," I explained clearly. "It's called modified duration, and it provides insight into how much a bond's price could change in response to interest rate changes."

Daadu found the new term intriguing and leaned forward. Meera, an observant onlooker, watched the interaction and appreciated the evolving layers of financial wisdom.

"Modified duration helps you understand how interest rate changes can impact your bond investments," I explained. "In simple terms, it indicates how much a bond's price is expected to change with a 1% change in interest rates. A bond or a debt fund with a higher modified duration will be more sensitive to interest rate changes, leading to more significant price fluctuations with rate hikes or drops."

Daadu, absorbing the explanation, nodded. "So, in the face of rising interest rates, as we're experiencing with the repo rate hikes, my debt funds with higher modified durations would be more adversely affected?"

"Exactly," I affirmed, "That's why modified duration is a crucial factor for investors to consider, especially in an environment where interest rates are expected to rise. It can help in constructing a portfolio with the desired risk exposure to interest rate movements."

Daadu was lost in thought, the room falling silent as he processed the new information. "How can one use this 'duration' to minimize risk?" he inquired, showing complete dedication to learning.

"When investing in debt funds, it's wise to diversify across various durations depending on your risk tolerance and investment horizon. When interest rates are rising, bonds with shorter durations are less affected by price movements but usually provide lower yields. Conversely, longer-duration bonds offer higher yields but are more responsive to changes in interest rates in terms of their price."

Daadu's expression, a combination of contemplation and appreciation, reflected his understanding: "It's a balancing act, managing risk while seeking returns, also how these instruments react to the market's pulse."

"Agreed," I said, feeling pleased that his point was understood. "It's important to stay informed, keep an eye on market trends, and understand that metrics like modified duration are tools to help navigate the wide range of investment options."

Daadu had just learned about yield and coupons, which made him curious about another aspect of financial markets. He asked me, "I often see short-term interest rates higher than longer-term ones. Shouldn't it be the opposite, since longer commitments should bring higher returns?"

Recognizing the complexity and significance of Daadu's question, I paused to think before answering. "That's a very astute observation, Daadu," I replied, admiration evident in my voice. "What you're referring to is an 'inverted yield curve,' and it's a phenomenon that economists and investors watch closely because it can signal shifts in the economic outlook."

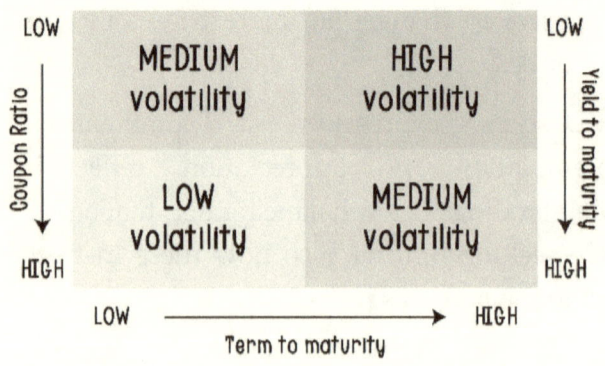

I continued, "Under normal circumstances, you're right. Longer-term investments typically offer higher returns to compensate for the increased risk. This is known as the 'term premium'. However, when short-term interest rates are higher than long-term rates, investors believe the near-term holds more uncertainty or risk than the future. This could be due to various factors, including expectations of economic slowdown or anticipations of monetary policy actions by central banks."

Daadu listened intently, taking in every word before nodding slowly. "So, it's not just about the passage of time, but rather the market's anticipations of what that time will bring," he reflected, feeling like he had finally grasped a crucial piece of the puzzle.

Meera observed the interaction in silence as she absorbed the weight of this revelation. Daadu, in turn, was both interested and somewhat worried about the implications of such market behaviors.

"However, it's important to remember," I added, noticing the concern in the room, "That an inverted yield curve doesn't directly cause economic problems, and there isn't a recession every time it happens. It's simply one of the lead indicators investors use to understand what might happen in the economy.

"Talking about this, I find it interesting to learn that the yield curve can have different shapes. Each shape gives us insights into the economy and how investors are feeling. Let's look at the three main shapes it can have.

"Normal Yield Curve: The normal yield curve, expected under typical economic conditions, slopes upward, reflecting higher yields for bonds with longer maturities. This indicates an expected growth in the economy, with inflation likely increasing over time. Investors demand higher returns for longer-term investments due to the greater risk of inflation and the uncertainty over a more extended period."

Daadu nodded, reflecting on his previous realization that making longer commitments should result in higher returns. This concept fits well with the idea of a typical yield curve.

"Lastly, there's the flat yield curve, which occurs when the yields on short-term and long-term bonds are very close, making the curve appear flat. This shape can indicate a transitional period in the economy, where investors are uncertain about future growth or inflation. It could mean that the economy is moving from a period of growth to slower growth or even a recession, or it could signal a recovery phase where interest rates are expected to rise."

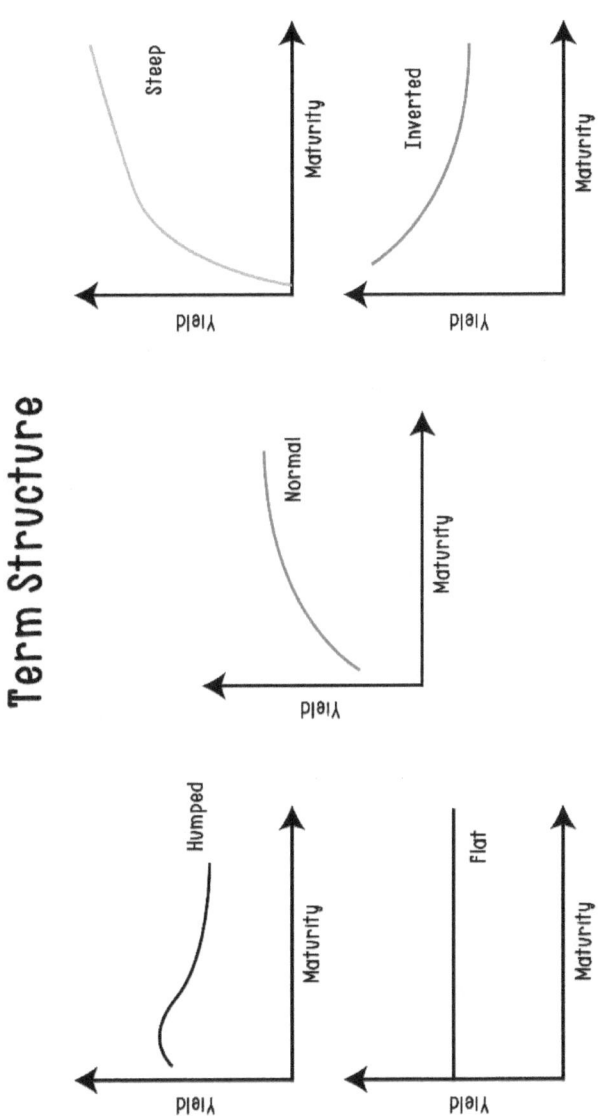

As the evening went on, we talked about fixed income and bonds. We moved from talking about theoretical ideas to practical investment strategies. We were all getting along well, sharing our thoughts and getting closer as a family through our discussions. After talking about different economic topics, we were about to conclude it with a rather eventful ending. Meera was an active participant in the conversation. However, she couldn't help but notice the shift in the atmosphere as the pace began to ease. Our eyes met, and in that instant, an unspoken understanding passed between us. It was a moment we had been thinking of, and it was finally happening.

With a small nod from Meera, I stood up from the table, signalling Daadu and Meera's father with a respectful smile that spoke of my gratitude for the evening's lessons. Daadu, sensing the unspoken exchange between us, offered a knowing smile and a gentle nod that conveyed his blessing without a word being spoken.

I reached out to Meera and asked her to come outside with me. We left the cosy family gathering and walked together hand in hand to the garden. It was quiet outside, and we could smell the jasmine and the fresh air after the rain.

In the serene garden, I faced Meera with sincerity. "Meera," I spoke gently, "As we discussed investments and risks tonight, it brought to mind the most important investment of all—our relationship."

While we stood close together in the quiet garden, I felt the ring in my pocket—a symbol of the deep love I have for Meera. The evening's conversations had only made me more certain of what I wanted. This was the moment, the perfect time to promise her the future we had always dreamed of.

I pulled back a little, my eyes locking with Meera's, where I could see endless possibilities and a deep, burning desire. I took a deep breath, the scent of jasmine mixing with the intensity of the moment. Then, slowly, I knelt before her, letting her feel how much she meant to me.

"Meera," I began, my voice steady but full of emotion, "Tonight, with everything we've shared and the love around us, I've never been more sure of anything. You are my guide when things are unclear, my steady support in a world that keeps changing."

I reached into my pocket and took out the ring, knowing the intensity of the future it held. I held it out to her, the silver band shining in the light, and asked, "Meera, will you marry me? Will you be my partner, my closest friend, and the greatest adventure of my life? With you, I have found a love that remains constant through all of life's ups and downs. Every moment with you is better. Together, let's build our future through both the good times and the tough ones."

Meera looked down at me, her eyes shining with tears of happiness, and my heart felt like it might burst with love. With no hesitation, she softly whispered, "Yes, Arjun. Yes, I will marry you. There's nothing I want more than to share my life with you and be by your side through whatever the future brings."

At that moment, everything felt like it had stopped. The garden, the stars, and the night seemed to celebrate with us, with their gentle swaying to the breeze. I slipped the ring onto her finger, and it fit perfectly as if it was always meant to be there. We hugged, our hearts in sync, with an unspoken promise to stay together forever.

As we walked back to the house hand in hand, the warm light from the windows spilt into the night, welcoming us. We weren't just two people in love; we were a couple ready to begin the biggest adventure of our lives together. So, this chapter of our lives didn't end but started a new one, with a promise of many more filled with love, laughter, and everything in between. Meera and I were beginning our own love story, where our hearts beat together, building a future side by side. This was the start of our forever, a love story that would always be remembered.

Disclaimers

Fictional Elements: "This book contains fictional narratives intended for entertainment and illustrative purposes. The characters, events, and dialogues are products of imagination. Any resemblance to real persons, living or dead, or actual events is purely coincidental."

Personal Views: "The views and opinions expressed in this book are solely those of the author and do not necessarily reflect the views or positions of any organization, employer, or entity associated with the author."

No Professional Advice: "The financial information and advice contained in this book are for educational purposes only and do not constitute professional financial, legal, or investment advice. Readers are advised to consult a qualified financial advisor or professional before making financial decisions."

No Liability: "The author and publisher disclaim all liability for any losses or damages incurred from using the information provided in this book. The information is provided 'as is' without guarantees of completeness, accuracy, or timeliness."

Best Efforts and Accuracy: "Best efforts have been put into covering all possible concepts and maintaining accuracy in this book; however, it is not a textbook. Readers are encouraged to conduct their own research to supplement the information provided."

Independent Research: "Readers are encouraged to conduct their own independent research and due diligence before making any financial or investment decisions, as the information provided in this book may not reflect current market conditions."

www.ingramcontent.com/pod-product-compliance
Lightning Source LLC
LaVergne TN
LVHW041613070526
838199LV00052B/3131